THE WEAVING OF HEARTS

Worship Resources For 17 Special Occasions

BY CYNTHIA E. COWEN

C.S.S Publishing Co., Inc.
Lima, Ohio

THE WEAVING OF HEARTS

Library of Congress Cataloging-in-Publication Data

Dowen, Cynthia E., 1947-
    The weaving of hearts : worship resources for 17 special occasions / by Cynthia E. Cowen.
        p.   c.m.
    ISBN 1-55673-392-5
    1. Occasional services.   I. Title.
BF199.03C68   1992
264—dc20   91-38336
                                                                              CIP

9210 / ISBN 1-55673-392-5   PRINTED IN U.S.A.

—■———————————————————————■—

To my parents, Edwin and Marjorie Ann Apelgren, whose faithfulness in exposing their family to Christ and his church "wove our hearts" together in love. As parents they give their love without asking for anything in return. Their support and encouragement have helped me to continue in my desire to share God's love through the written word. May this resource reflect their love and mine as we are all "woven together" in Christ's love, in his body, the church.

—■———————————————————————■—

Table Of Contents

Cut, Broken, Stirred And Healed

A Service Of Reconciliation

WELCOME AND INSTRUCTIONS

CALL TO RESTORED FELLOWSHIP:

Most Holy God, We call upon you to be present weaving our hearts with yours in thanksgiving for your loving mercy shown to us through Christ Jesus our Lord. Shine your light into the darkness of our souls that we, who have been alienated from you through sin, might be restored to wholeness once more. Be present, Holy Spirit, stirring our hearts to respond in this time of fellowship and learning. We, who have been cut off from you through sin, broken in that knowledge, stirred up through repentance, and healed by grace and love, come before you now in adoration and praise.

C: Come, Holy Spirit. Amen.

CUT OFF FROM GOD

L: As creatures of God, we were not always alienated from our Creator. Hear what the Word of God has to say about what God created and saw as good.

Reading: Genesis 1:11-12

C: Your fruit and seed were good, O Great Creator God.

Reading: Genesis 2:8-9

C: Your garden and seed were good, O Great Creator God.

Reading: Genesis 2:15-22

C: Your Word and creations were good, O Great Creator God.

L: What God created as good became bruised by sin and disobedience to his Word.

Reading: Genesis 3:1-7

C: We bring to you, O Merciful Lord, lives cut deep by sin as we are reminded of the taste of forbidden fruit.

Offering of Fruit: Participants lift their fruit, slice into fourths, and eat a section.

L: Having eaten of the fruit of our sin, we turn our attention to our need for repentance. Hear what God's Word has to say about this.

Reading: Matthew 3:1-10

C: O Reconciling Lord, our paths have been prepared by your spirit to lead us to true repentance. The axe has fallen on the root of sin in our lives. Cut down, we ask your cleansing fire upon the chaff of our lives that the seeds of your love will grow within the gardens of our hearts.

Reading: Galatians 5:22-24

C: Sanctifying Spirit, we are crucified with Christ and raised to new life through belief in him. Bring forth your fruit.

Reading: John 15:1-11

C: Our joy is now full.

Special Musical Offering

BROKEN FOR SERVICE

L: Having tasted of the fruit of sin, receive forgiveness, and allow God to create the fruit of his Spirit within. Come now before the Lord to feed upon him that we might become broken of self and healed to be food for others. Hear the Word of the Lord.

Reading: Deuteronomy 8:1-10

C: We've wandered the desert of disobedience too long, O Guiding Light. Feed us with the living bread of life so that we will hunger no more. Open our mouths to receive.

Reading: Psalm 51:15-17

C: We offer to you a sacrifice of broken spirits and contrite hearts.

Reading: John 6:33-40

Offering of Bread: Participant lifts bread.

Reading: 1 Corinthians 11:23-26

C: We remember your sacrifice, O Bread Of Life.

L: We respond to our need to be fed through the prayer Christ taught us to pray:

Lord's Prayer

STIRRED TO NEW LIFE

L: God has seen his people eat the bread of affliction and in his mercy has provided a land flowing with milk and honey. Hear his promise to us, his chosen people.

Reading: Exodus 3:7-8

C: We hunger and thirst for new life, O Lord.

Reading: Isaiah 55:1-2

C: **We hunger and thirst for new life, O Lord.**

Reading: 1 Peter 2:1-3

C: **Satisfy our thirst with your milk, O Lord.**

Offering of Milk: Participant lifts milk.

L: Our God adds to this milk the sweetness of his Word.

Reading: Psalm 119:103-104

C: **We desire to taste of honey, O Nourishing Spirit.**

Reading: Isaiah 7:14-15

C: **We choose to eat of your honeycomb, O Blest Provider.**

Offering of Honey: Participant lifts the honey.

Reading: Psalm 34:7-10

C: **We come to taste of your milk and honey, Blessed Nourisher of our souls.**

L: As we gather today to break bread in this meal, let us remember our brokenness which is restored through fellowship with God and with one another. As we drink the milk, let us remember our craving for the true spiritual milk of God. As we add the honey to our bread or milk, let us remember the sweetness of God's Word. God leads us into the Promised Land, a land flowing with milk and honey, through Christ Jesus our Lord. Break bread now in fellowship with God and one another to show your brokenness healed and willingness to be used of God. Dipped in his love and in his promises, be nourished in spirit.

C: **We come to satisfy our thirst with new life. We eat to satisfy our hunger for you, Blest Lord and giver of eternal life.**

HEALED IN HIS LOVE

L: Fed by the Spirit, we now feed the body. Bless our food to enable it to nourish the soul as we reach out to those who have not yet tasted of God's love and mercy.

C: **May the world be made whole in Christ Jesus our Lord. Amen.**

Fellowship Meal and Program

In Honor Of Mother

A Service For Mother's Day

Today we honor the "mother." Everyone who is present has a biological mother, but one may be a "mother" without being a natural mother. Hear what Christ had to say concerning his family:

"While Jesus was still talking to the crowd, his mother and brothers stood outside, wanting to speak to him. Someone told him, 'Your mother and brothers are standing outside, wanting to speak to you.'

"He replied to him, 'Who is my mother, and who are my brothers?'

"Pointing to his disciples, he said, 'Here are my mother and my brothers. For whoever does the will of my Father in heaven is my brother and sister and mother.' "— Luke 12:46-50

And so, today we honor those who have been given the opportunity to mother, physically or spiritually, as we offer our praise and thanksgiving to the Father for the gifts he gives mothers in carrying out their responsibility.

A LITANY IN HONOR OF MOTHERS

L: O God, we celebrate the role of the mothers in our lives.

C: Thank you for women who have touched us with your love, all caring God.

L: We praise you, O God, for mothers who set children and family above possessions,

C: Thank you for those who sacrifice to stay in the home.

L: We praise you, O God, for mothers who provide for the needs of their families.

C: **Bless those who work outside the home with special opportunities to share their love.**

L: We praise you for the lives of women in our midst who set good examples with right moral values and serve you in true dedication.

C: **Thank you for mothers who give us right teaching and guidance for living.**

L: As Sarah laughed at the thought of being a mother at her advanced age,

C: **We laugh at our inadequacies to mother.**

L: As Pharaoh's daughter took baby Moses into her home embracing him as her own,

C: **We take all your children into our hearts.**

L: As Samson's mother taught him God's ways,

C: **We set our hearts on you as we train others in your ways.**

L: As Hannah nurtured her small son, Samuel, and then released him to live in your temple,

C: **We release our children into your care.**

L: As Mary pondered the angel's announcement of the birth of the Christ,

C: **We are awestruck at the thought of the very life of Christ being planted within us.**

L: As Jairus' wife stayed behind to pray over her sick child,

C: **We offer our prayers for the family.**

L: God gives us the gift of faith and asks us to share that gift with others.

C: **Bless mothers everywhere as they plant the faith of Christ within hungry hearts.**

L: Our spirits rejoice that as we do the will of the Father we become the brothers, sisters, and mother of our Lord and Savior Jesus the Christ.

C: **We praise you for that blessed honor. Amen.**

Prayer:

Bless, O Lord, those in our midst who are committed to serving you in the role of a mother either physically or spiritually. Give them abundant love as they reach out to all your children — their own and those of our church family and those of the world. Stir up within their hearts the gifts of compassion, healing, laughter, tears, joy, strength, commitment and faith that they will reflect the life of Christ Jesus within.

As your son looked upon the face of Mary his mother in love, look upon the faces of these precious mothers we honor today. In Christ's name, we pray.

C: **Amen.**

Optional Celebration: Presentation of mothers in the congregation with a flower or a gift made for them by children of the Sunday school.

Wording of presentation: In celebration of "Mother," we at *(name of church)* wish to bless those in our midst who hold the love of Jesus as a mother in their hearts. All who are grandmothers, mothers or spiritual mothers are asked to receive a *(flower/gift)* as a symbol of the blessing that Christ Jesus has given you.

This part of the presentation does not have to be copied onto the order of service. The service may be used as an insert to the morning worship service bulletin *(two sides)* and inserted into the order of worship where the leader feels appropriate.

A Memorial Day Remembrance

A Service For Memorial Day

Memorial Day began as a time set aside to remember those who had fallen in battle during the Civil War. A group of women, in order to honor those who had died that year, decorated graves in remembrance of that sacrifice. May 30, 1868, officially set that time apart as an observance across our nation. Years passed, wars continued, and the tradition of remembering those who had died began to establish this day in the heart. Today most people tend to look at Memorial Day as a three-day weekend, a time to gather with family, have a picnic or barbecue, rest, fix up the yard, and make a quick run to the cemetery to put some flowers on the grave of someone lost through death.

This Memorial Day let us refocus our attention and center in on Christ, the One who has given us hope in eternal life. Out of respect and tribute to the departed, we look to Jesus who has gone before us to prepare an eternal home for all those who die believing in him.

And so we remember today: those who have died serving their country, those loved ones we miss who have died in the faith, and Jesus who died that we would be united through faith when our time comes to join our Savior and the saints.

Let us ask God to weave our hearts to his as we share in this special litany of remembrance.

(Option: This section does not have to be included on the bulletin insert. Leader may read this as introductory comments before beginning the litany.)

A LITANY IN HONOR OF MEMORIAL DAY

L: In praise for the sacrifice of your precious body and blood,

C: Weave our hearts in remembrance, O Lord.

L: In tribute of those who founded our nation and the faith upon which she was built,

C: Weave our hearts in remembrance, O Lord.

L: In respect for those who died in defense of our country and its honor,

C: Weave our hearts in remembrance, O Lord.

L: In gratitude to our Lord for the assurance that we shall be united in faith with loved ones again,

C: Weave our hearts in remembrance, O Lord.

L: Let us pause in silence now to remember Jesus whose sacrifice liberated us from the bondage of sin and death and to remember those who died that our nation might enjoy the gift of liberty.

(Time of silence)
Taps
Solo

L: Grant us true freedom in you, O God, that we might continue to enjoy our country's heritage. The price for the freedoms we enjoy is costly as was our freedom through Christ costly to you. May justice and peace be preserved and extended to your hurting and needy world.

C: Amen.

In Honor Of Father

A Service For Father's Day

Father's Day, a day set aside in honor of "father."

Jesus taught in the Lord's Prayer to address God as Father, "Our Father who art in heaven, hallowed be thy name (Matthew 6:9)." God the Father desires that we honor our heavenly Father and our earthly fathers. In fact, this is the one commandment that carries with it a blessing: "Honor your father and your mother, so that you may live long in the land the Lord your God is giving you (Exodus 20:12)."

Christ was one with his father: "I and the Father are one (John 10:30)," and "No one comes to the Father except through me (John 14:6)," Christ told his followers.

When we know Jesus, we know our Heavenly Father. When we know Jesus, we honor and forgive our earthly fathers for no one person is perfect. This is not a day to preach at fathers by exhorting them to be something they may not be able to be. This is not a day to place a heavy burden upon fathers by reminding them of their responsibilities as a parent. This is not a day to embarrass fathers by laying on them gushy garlands of praise and sentimentality. This is a day to remember the love of our Abba Father and honor the relationship he had with his own child, Jesus, and which he desires to have with each of us, his own children.

We now join in that celebration recognizing the love of God made perfect through Christ Jesus as children of the Heavenly Father. We take this time to honor our natural fathers and glorify our Father in heaven with a litany of appreciation.

(Option: This part of the service does not need to be printed on the bulletin insert. The leader may use it as an introduction to the litany to be read.)

19

A LITANY IN HONOR OF FATHERS

L: In appreciation for the role of the father,

C: **Our hearts look to you, O Lord.**

L: For the right guidance and direction we have received in life from our dad,

C: **Our hearts give thanks.**

L: For the happy memories of times shared in fun and fellowship,

C: **Our hearts give thanks.**

L: For the hard lessons dad let us learn as we took responsibility for our own actions,

C: **Our hearts give thanks.**

L: For being there when we needed you, dad,

C: **Our hearts give thanks.**

L: For not being there we forgive,

C: **May our hearts be healed.**

L: In appreciation for the strength needed during every stage of our life,

C: **Our hearts look to you, O Lord.**

L: For being the rock we could climb to during the storm,

C: **Father, we thank you.**

L: For providing our daily bread and clothing,

C: Father, we thank you.

L: For the laughter and tears, for the hugs and the understanding quiet,

C: Father, we thank you.

L: Heavenly Father, as you loved your son, Jesus, look upon us, your children, in that love. Look upon our fathers and bless them. In their successes rejoice and smile. In their failures grant understanding and forgiveness. All praise be to you, Almighty Father, for the vastness of your love that will always be constant for us and for our fathers. In your name we pray.

C: Amen.

Blanket Sunday

A Service To Recognize Relief Workers

HYMN: "Praise and Thanksgiving"

WE RESPOND TO CHRIST'S LOVE
BY REACHING OUT TO OTHERS

Leader: The book of Acts tells us that the first church came together after hearing the good news about Jesus to devote themselves to study, fellowship, the breaking of bread, and prayer. One of the manifestations of this encounter with the reality of Jesus Christ as Lord was that many were filled with awe as they saw wonders and miraculous signs being performed. The Word tells us that "All the believers were together and had everything in common. Selling their possessions and goods, they gave to anyone as he or she had a need (Acts 2:44-45)." This is truly good news for us today as we see the love of Christ being manifested for others in response to receiving that love personally.

On this Blanket Sunday we come together to honor the love and donations which have gone into the items you now see before you. These completed works have been brought to God to be blessed. All year round our ladies have gathered to cut, piece, and sew materials together to create quilts to be given to those in need in our community and throughout the world. Articles have been donated to create health care kits, school kits, and layettes which also will be given to those in need. Outreach to the needy is an important ministry of the church. All benefit from the love and care shared with others, the giver and the receiver.

We read in Acts 9 of a disciple named Tabitha (Dorcas). She was always doing good and helping the poor. When she died the Apostle Peter was asked to visit. The mourners took

23

him upstairs where all the widows stood around him, crying and showing him the robes and other clothing that Dorcas had made for others while alive. Many churches have Dorcas' Circles. The name honors the one who gave to others out of a heart responding to the love she experienced in Jesus Christ.

(Option: This part of the service need not be printed on the bulletin if space is limited. It may be used as an introduction to the litany.)

DEDICATION OF QUILTS AND KITS

L: We set aside this part of our worship to celebrate and ask God's blessing upon these quilts and kits which are now being offered up as gifts of love for those in need. Join us now as we rejoice in the fruit of a labor of love.

C: We offer our gifts of love to the God of Love.

L: Lord, we present to you these quilts and blankets which will bring warmth to the body as well as to the soul.

C: Bless these gifts, O Lord.

L: Lord, you welcomed the children holding them on your knees so you could love and instruct them. Look with favor upon these school kits which will enable eager minds to have tools with which to study.

C: Bless these gifts, O Lord.

L: Lord, you care about our personal needs. Thank you for the basic necessities which these health care kits will provide for those who do not have what we take for granted.

C: Bless these gifts, O Lord.

L: Lord, you came as a tiny child into this world. The stable which was your birthing room, the straw which was your bedding, the swaddling clothes which your mother Mary wrapped you in, all remind us of your choice to give up cozy sleepers, warm blankets, and a heated nursery for us. Bless these layettes which will bring joy to mothers and fathers who hold a precious gift of life.

C: **Bless these gifts, O Lord.**

WE RELEASE THE WORKS OF OUR HANDS TO THE WORKING OF GOD'S

L: Let us pray.

Prayer: Lord Jesus, out of hearts responding in love to your sacrifice for us, we have presented the works of our hands and asked your blessing upon them. (Place a quilt, health care kit, school kit, and layette upon the altar.) Receive them now as we release them into your hands. May our brothers and sisters in our community and throughout the world feel your love as they are given these special gifts. We rejoice at having the opportunity to share with those in need through this ministry of our women within the church. We pray in your wonderful name.

C: **Amen.**

HYMN: "Praise God, from Whom All Blessings Flow"

LEADER'S HELPS

This service is designed to be a blessing service for those congregations who participate in preparing quilts, blankets, layettes, school kits, health care kits, for the needy in their community and the world. Decorate the sanctuary on a special Sunday with a sampling of these items. A display of items and pictures may be arranged in the narthex for people to examine. The entire service can be printed on a bulletin insert or just the dedication service.

(Options: Recognize the women and number of items made and worked on throughout the year. Incorporate a temple talk on the church relief agencies at the beginning of worship.)

Hearts Warmed With Thanksgiving

A Thanksoffering Service Of Light

INVOCATION

Lord of the light, we come to you mindful of the darkness that surrounds us in this world. Shine your light into our midst as we offer to you our time, our possessions, our very beings, signs of your gracious love. Be present now, warming our hearts with thanksgiving.

C: Kindle in us the fire of your love.

HYMN: "Immortal, Invisible, God Only Wise"

THE LIGHT BEGINS TO SHINE

L: Lord of Light, we come before you knowing that darkness exists in our souls. Shine your light deep within, purging our inner beings from all sin.

C: Let there be light in our midst.
(Candle #1 is lit.)

L: Lord of Light, we feel the darkness that surrounds our families in an evil world. Protect us all as you shine your light from us to our natural and extended family members. Encircle us now and the ones we love with the arc of your love.

C: Let there be light in our midst.
(Candle #2 is lit.)

L: Lord of Light, we need your light to shine within our community so that all who are struggling, who are in need of employment, who are treated unfairly, who are assisting others through education and fellowship, who are seeking a better environment for all to live in, will see that your light does dispel the darkness.

C: Let there be light in our midst.
(Candle #3 is lit.)

THE FIRE IS FANNED THROUGH FAITH

Candle #1 The Father

L: Father, having lit this first candle to you, we are mindful of the words you spoke at creation: "Let there be light," and light appeared.
(Waves hand over Candle #1.)

C: Appear in our midst, O Lord.

Candle #2 The Son

L: Jesus Christ, this second candle reminds us that you came as a light to the world saying, "I am the light of the world. Whoever follows me will never walk in darkness, but will have the light of life."
(Waves hand over Candle #2.)

C: Appear in our midst, O Lord.

Candle #3 The Holy Spirit

L: Holy Spirit, our third candle shines brightly in acknowledgment that you enlighten our hearts revealing the Father through the Son. You make his light shine in our hearts to give us the light of the knowledge of the glory of God in the face of Christ.
(Waves hand over Candle #3.)

C: Appear in our midst, O Lord.

WARMED HEARTS RESPOND WITH THANKSGIVING

L: As we have lit three candles asking God's light and love to shine into our hearts, our family situations, our community, and our very spirits, let us now respond as we bring our offerings before his throne that his light through the church can continue to go out to a dark and needy world.

HYMN: "God Himself is Present"

OFFERING *(Individuals may come forward to table area where the three candles are and place their offerings in basket or upon table.)*

SPECIAL MUSICAL OFFERING

THE LIGHT CONTINUES TO WARM AND GROW

L: Having asked the Father, Son and Spirit to be present with us, we lift our offerings up before the Eternal Light of Heaven. Bathe these humble gifts, Almighty God, in the light of your blessing. Receive them to further the work of your kingdom. Multiply them for your use as they touch others.

C: **May our light encourage all who live in darkness as it spreads the good news of the love of Christ Jesus our Lord throughout the land. Amen.**

A FINAL TOUCH TO THE HEART

BENEDICTION

L: Go forth from here with God's blessing, swinging the lamp of faith as it lights each pathway through a dark and dangerous world. Rejoice in the light of the Spirit which ignites the heart with love. Respond with thanksgiving to the one true light, Jesus Christ, as you shine to all around. In

29

his name, be lights yourselves to those you encounter as you journey from here to place your light with all the others of faith before the throne of God. In the name of the Father, the Son, and the Holy Spirit.

C: Amen.
(Candles are extinguished.)

HYMN: "Praise God From Whom All Blessings Flow"

A Weaving Of Worship

A Service Of Communion

THE FABRIC OF OUR LIFE EXAMINED

P: Coming before a God who loves us, we confess that we have not taken care of the fabric of our being as we should. We begin our worship with prayerful and honest examination.

(Silence for reflection)

Confession

L: We stand before you with fabric soiled by sin, All Knowing God. We confess that we have sinned in thought, in word, and in action toward you and toward each other.

C: Cleanse us, All Loving God.

L: For the times that we have neglected our communion with you through prayer and the reading of your word,

C: Cleanse us, All Loving God.

L: For the broken threads of trust which we have allowed to snap between our brothers and sisters in faith and with those around us in family, work, and the church,

C: Cleanse us, All Loving God.

L: For the unraveling of relationships between those closest to us,

C: Cleanse us, All Loving God.

L: For those times when we have felt neglected by our family and when we have neglected to meet their needs,

C: **Cleanse us, All Loving God.**

L: For those times when we have resented the work load, the loneliness, the stresses of dealing with people, the financial struggles, the pain of life,

C: **Cleanse us, All Loving God.**

L: For those times when we have looked with envy upon what others have and have been blinded to our own blessings,

C: **Cleanse us, All Loving God.**

L: Take the material we now present to you, All Caring God, and cleanse it through the blood of Jesus Christ our Lord.

C: **Though our sins be as scarlet, they will be white as snow; though they are red as crimson, they shall be like wool.**

Absolution

L: God cleanses us through the sacrifice of his beloved Son. Receive the forgiveness of your sins as you are washed in the blood and presented to God pure and spotless, cleansed materials to be used in his loving hands.

THE LOOM IS PREPARED

Call To Worship

L: Having been cleansed from all sin, let us now call upon God to prepare the looms of our hearts in order to worship him. We gather together as individuals to enable the Holy Spirit to weave us together as we worship the Creator of Life.

We rejoice that it is God who takes our individual life strips and connects them to others to form a pattern for life lived out in community. Let us be bound to God through Christ and to each other in his love.

C: Send your spirit of worship, Awesome God.

Opening Hymn: "Take My Life"

GOD'S MATERIAL LAID OUT

First Lesson

Psalm

Anthem

Second Lesson

Alleluia

The Gospel Announced

Gospel Lesson

The Gospel Of The Lord

A PATTERN DISPLAYED

Sermon

THE DESIGN ENHANCED THROUGH PRAISE

Hymn: "For the Beauty of the Earth"

CONNECTED THROUGH FAITH IN CHRIST

Creed

Prayers Of The Church

Sharing Of The Peace

WE SEW INTO THE FABRIC OUR OFFERINGS

Offering

A Special Musical Weaving

Offertory

Prayer

L: Almighty Creator, your people give you thanks for all your gifts bestowed upon us since the beginning of time. You delicately spun the stars attaching them to the heavens. The fleecy clouds were lovingly combed by your gentle fingers. Darkness was replaced with the brilliance of light as the planets were hung in orbit around the sun. A garment of life was then produced as the earth became filled with your majestic creativity. All of creation bows before you in praise and adoration.

C: We praise you, Great Creator.

The Great Thanksgiving

L: The Lord be with you.

C: And also with you.

L: Lift up your hearts.

C: We lift them up unto the Lord our God.

L: Let us give thanks to our Creator.

C: It is right to give God thanks and praise.

L: The cloak woven at creation is many colored, fields plush with the green of vegetation, sparkling blue waters, diverse creatures of land and seas. All your wonders unite to sing your praise, Great Designer of All.

C: **All creation seeks warmth and shelter.** We draw near now to you, O God, and to one another in the celebration of communion to receive that embracing protection. The world with its variety of patterns calls to us to be divided, but in Christ we are woven into a divine pattern strengthened for his service through this blessed sacrament we are about to receive and made one.

L: God, as you spin and weave upon the loom of love, all your creations marvel at your great design. Your works proclaim your goodness!

THE TABLE PREPARED

L: When Jesus walked upon this earth, he spread his cloak of truth revealing the kingdom of God. His garments of righteousness convicted those who had soiled their own by sin. Power was vested in every part of his being for to touch the hem of his garment brings healing today as it did then. As Christ Jesus, our Lord, prepared his last supper for his followers, so he now prepares us to feast with him in holy communion.

C: **Come, Lord Jesus.**

Words Of Institution

L: On the night of his betrayal, Jesus took bread, gave thanks, and broke it giving it to his disciples saying, "This is my body, given for you; do this in remembrance of me." Now as we eat this bread and drink this cup, we proclaim the Lord's death until he comes again.

C: **As we receive the body and blood of Jesus Christ, may we be his body to the world. As we are empowered by the spirit, may we begin to weave new patterns of justice to all by the truth which Christ has revealed to us in his Word.**

Enable us to reach out to cover the naked, feed the hungry, bind up the wounds of the suffering with strips of compassion, and put on garments of joy bringing hope to a hurting world. We feast now on Christ in remembrance.

L: Let it be. Come, Lord Jesus, and clothe us in your righteousness with the garments of forgiveness and humility.

C: Come, Lord Jesus.

Lord's Prayer

Distribution Of Communion

GOD'S WEAVING CONTINUES

L: Let us pray. Strengthened now through the body and blood of Christ Jesus, our Lord, we go forth to unite with our family, friends, co-workers, community, and others in this world to live out God's design for our lives. May our ties be secure in him as the pattern continues to grow and mesh with those of his kingdom.

C: His perfect will be done in our lives. Amen.

Benediction

Closing Hymn: "Sent Forth By God's Blessing"

Weaving A Tapestry Of Worship

A Service Of Communion

THE CALL TO BEGIN TO WEAVE OUR WORSHIP

L: We call upon the name of the one who stood at creation and wove a wonderful work. Marvelous things were created through the spoken word. Each creation was unique in the hands of the Weaver. With tender love we were formed and cared for. Standing back, the Creator God looked at the finished tapestry of life and was very pleased.

We come now to offer back to him a time of worship for the creation of our individual lives, for the weaving of those lives with those we share in community with, and for extending our lives to connect with all who live in this world of awesome design.

Intertwined with one another through Christ Jesus our Lord, we ask the Holy Spirit now to bind us together in a spirit of love and worship.

Opening Hymn: "God Whose Almighty Word"

THE WEAVER BEGINS TO WORK

L: We stand before the loom upon which we see our lives created. The Cross is God's loom upon which the sin-broken threads of our lives are mended in Christ, the Divine Weaver. Confessing our sins, the tapestries of our lives are then healed and woven together as the body of Christ.

C: Mend our brokenness, O Lord.

L: We confess our stubbornness, Almighty God. We acknowledge that we at times pursue our own lines of interest instead of allowing you to guide the flow of our lives.

C: Mend our brokenness, O Lord.

L: We confess our failure at furnishing good materials in our lives for you to work with, Holy Spirit. We acknowledge that we at times neglect to commune with you in prayer or be attended to you through your Word.

C: Mend our brokenness, O Lord.

L: We confess our blindness, Jesus, as people who stumble and fall in the hurt and pain of living out daily life. We acknowledge that we at times allow circumstances in life to overwhelm us because of a lack of trust in the hand of the Designer.

C: Mend our brokenness, O Lord.

L: We confess our doubts at the way we see the patterns of life unfolding. We acknowledge that sickness, financial struggles, marital stress, wayward family, professional jealousy, overwhelming workloads, loneliness, and the like are not caused by you but that you take even these tattered pieces and weave them to strengthen the fabric of our beings.

C: Mend our brokenness, O Lord.

GOD MENDS US

L: God in mercy has heard our cries as we have placed them at the Cross of Christ. Receive forgiveness as you are set free from sin through the sacrifice of Christ. Children of a fallen humanity, we now rise as new creations through the waters of our baptism into the death and resurrection of Christ. We respond to the life of the Spirit as called and empowered disciples of Jesus our Lord.

C: Amen.

THE WORD IS WOVEN INTO OUR SPIRITS

First Lesson

Psalm

Dancers Continue the Design or Special Music

Second Lesson

Alleluia

The Gospel Announced

The Gospel

The Gospel of the Lord

GOD'S PATTERN IS REVEALED

Sermon

WE WEAVE OUR VOICES IN PRAISE

Hymn: "Let All Things Now Living"

ONE TAPESTRY THROUGH FAITH IN CHRIST

Creed

L: Do you believe in God, the Creator?

C: I believe in God, the Father Almighty, Creator of heaven and earth. I believe that I am the work of his hands!

L: Do you believe in Jesus Christ?

C: I believe in Jesus Christ, his only Son, our Lord. He was conceived by the power of the Holy Spirit and born of the Virgin Mary. He suffered under Pontius Pilate, was crucified, died and was buried. He descended into Hell. On the third day he rose again. He ascended into Heaven, and is seated at the right hand of the Father. He will come again to judge the living and the dead. I believe that I am woven into Christ through his death and resurrection.

L: Do you believe in the Holy Spirit?

C: **I believe in the Holy Spirit, the holy Catholic Church, the communion of saints, the forgiveness of sins, the resurrection of the body, and the life everlasting. I believe that the fabric of my life is strengthened by the spirit, the church, and the fellowship of believers in Christ. In the blood of Christ my sins are cleansed, and I shall look forward to his coming and life eternal.**

WE WEAVE OUR PRAYERS BEFORE THE GREAT DESIGNER

L: We come before the one who knows the patterns of our lives and the needs of our hearts. We offer up to his perfect will the petitions of our hearts. Lord in your mercy,

C: **Hear our prayer.**
(Petitions from the body now lifted.)

L: Into your hands, Almighty God, we place these petitions trusting in your mercy as you so design.

C: **Amen.**

WE SHARE IN THE COMMON FABRIC OF LOVE

Sharing of the Peace

WE SOW IN THE KINGDOM OF STEWARDSHIP

Offering

Special Music Designed to be Shared

Offertory

THE LOOM CONTINUES TO REVEAL GOD'S PLAN

Tapestry Litany

L: T — TODAY we gather TO give THANKS TO a God we TRUST.

C: **Weave our hearts as one.**

L: A — ANNOUNCE our presence AT your table, ALL saving Christ,

C: **Weave our hearts as one.**

L: P — PRAISE we offer and thanks to our PROTECTOR and PROVIDER God,

C: **Weave our hearts as one.**

L: E — ETERNAL God who EASES our pain and grants EVERLASTING life,

C: **Weave our hearts as one.**

L: S — SUCH as we are, we SEEK our SALVATION through your SON our Lord and SAVIOR,

C: **Weave our hearts as one.**

L: T — TOGETHER we TRAVEL a journey THROUGH TIME, TIED and connected in love.

C: **Weave our hearts as one.**

L: R — RETURN soon, Great REDEEMER, to RESCUE your READY children,

C: **Weave our hearts as one.**

L: Y — YESTERDAY'S passed; tomorrow will come; today is YET with us. YOU, O Lord, are the reason for living and YOU alone satisfy the YEARNINGS of our souls,

C: **Weave our hearts as one.**

L: United as one in Christ Jesus, our Lord, we come to the table to be restored to him.

C: Amen.

THANKSGIVING CONNECTS US TO GOD

L: Let us pray: With our brokenness mended by grace, we rejoice in the wholeness of our spirits. Divine Weaver, your pattern for our lives is hidden from full view. We glimpse a corner here and there as the threads are intertwined with others to form a living garment which covers the world. The many textures and colors reflect the grandeur of the tapestry. We join with the faithful everywhere to give you our thanksgiving.

The Great Thanksgiving

L: Our God be with you.

C: And also with you.

L: Lift up your hearts.

C: We lift them up to God.

L: Let us give thanks to our Creator.

C: It is right to give God thanks and praise.

L: It is truly right to give God praise for the wonder of the workmanship displayed in all creation. The tapestry of life surrounding us reflects the intricacy of divine order. The fleecy clouds, the delicacy of a snowflake, the blossoms in Spring, the cycle of life and death for all creatures remind us that the hand of the Almighty is continually at work.

C: We acknowledge the great design of the universe and praise you for selecting us to be an integral part of an eternal design.

L: A basket of cloth strips stands before the loom. The hand of the weaver carefully selects those which will fit the design and give strength to the fabric.

C: **As the Samaritan bound up the wounds of the injured man on the road to Jericho, we reach out to bind the wounds of the hungry, the neglected, the unloved, the lost, and all your hurting creation with love, compassion, justice and service.**

L: We praise you for the focus of our eyes as we explore the unfolding garment before us. Jacob's cloak was designed in many colors. Jews, Samaritans, and people of other nations laid their cloaks down among the palms as you rode triumphantly into Jerusalem as their Messiah.

C: **We praise you for the uniqueness of every race and culture. We, too, sing your hosannas.**

Sanctus

THE TABLE PREPARED

Words of Preparation

L: In the night of our Lord's betrayal, Jesus took bread, gave thanks, broke it, and gave it to his disciples. "Take and eat," he said. "This is my body, given for you. Do this in remembrance of me."

After the meal, he again took the cup, gave thanks, and gave it to all to drink revealing a new plan. "This is the new covenant in my blood, shed for you and for all people for the forgiveness of sin. Do this in remembrance of me."

For as often as we eat of this bread and drink from this cup, we proclaim the Lord's death until he comes again.

C: **Christ has died. Christ is risen. Christ will come again!**

L: Therefore, Almighty God, with this bread and cup, we remember your birth and life, your sacrifice and death. We join with all who have been woven together in faith by Christ as witnesses to your resurrection and await your coming in power to share with us the great and promised feast.

C: Amen. Come, Lord Jesus.

L: Send now your Holy Spirit so that we and all who now share in your body and blood may receive new life and embrace our own death and resurrection through Christ.

C: Amen. Come, Lord Jesus.

L. Weave our prayers with those of your servants of every time and place, uniting them with the ceaseless petitions of our great high priest until he comes as victorious God of all.

C: Through him, with him, in him, in the unity of the Holy Spirit, all honor and glory is yours, Creator God, now and forever. Amen.

The Lord's Prayer

Distribution of Holy Communion
(Communion Hymns)

L: Strengthened to begin anew, we go forth from this service celebrating the pattern set before us as we are woven together in Christ.

C: Entwine our hearts as one in you, O Lord!

Benediction

Closing Hymn "Weave"

This service is designed to involve its participants in seeing that, as unique creations of God, we come together and bring our individual gifts to build up the body. We are woven together in Christ Jesus our Lord through faith. We are woven together in worship of God. We are woven together as we pool our resources to reach out to others.

The service, as written, involves a worship leader, a pastor, and the congregation. The pastor may do the entire service. Musical selections are suggested ending with "Weave" by Rosemary Crow, to which most congregations have access. There is an opportunity for liturgical dancers to be incorporated in the service. If there is no such group in the congregation or body using this resource, a musical number may be presented.

This service may be used as a special service for a congregation or group gathering outside the context of church for worship. It is ideal for a retreat or conference. The Tapestry Litany, communion, or other portions may be deleted to shorten the service.

As an option to enhancing the theme of the service, a special banner may be created. Participants can be asked ahead of time to make a cross out of material which they feel they are like. Some examples are: apple print for teacher, nursery print cotton for a mother, terry cloth for a crier, pictures of family, needlepoint. These crosses then can be attached to a large piece of banner material with a glue stick — many crosses pieced together to form God's design pointing to our uniqueness yet signifying our oneness.

If this is done in the church, each individual family unit may be mailed the pattern (possibly through the newsletter) and on that Sunday be asked to add their cross with name to the banner. Great for a stewardship push!

The crosses are all the same size as from this pattern and would piece together to make a very interesting banner or be attached to a large flannelgraph board or bulletin board in the narthex.

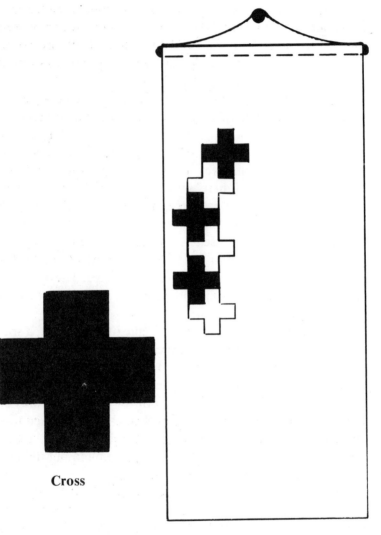

Cross

Banner

Installation Of Readers And Communion Assistants

A Service Of Commissioning

L: Today we recognize the ministry of those in our midst who have responded to God's call to serve as readers and communion assistants at our worship services. I would ask that those who have made a commitment to these two areas of ministry now come forward to be installed for this service within our congregational worship.
(Readers and communion assistants come forward.)

L: Hear what God's Word has to say about service through gifts of the Spirit: (Romans 12:4-9) "For as in one body we have many members, and not all the members have the same function, so we, who are many, are one body in Christ, and individually we are members one of another. We have gifts that differ according to the grace given to us: prophecy, in proportion to faith; ministry, in ministering; the teacher, in teaching; the exhorter, in exhortation; the giver, in generosity; the leader, in diligence; the compassionate, in cheerfulness."

L: You have responded to God's call to serve in the ministry of service among us through the reading of the Holy Scriptures and assisting with the distribution of Holy Communion. Do you promise to faithfully administer the Word and sacrament when called upon to do so?

C: Yes, and I ask God to help me.

L: All Scripture is inspired by God and is useful for teaching, for reproof, for correction, and for training in righteousness, so that everyone who belongs to God may be proficient, equipped for every good work. Do you promise to be faithful in your personal study of the word so that the Spirit will be able to give you understanding as you share it with others?

C: **Yes, and I ask the Spirit to help me.**

L: Jesus Christ is the Word made flesh. On the night in which he was betrayed, he shared the bread and wine which would become his body and blood given and shed for us for the remission of our sins through his atoning death upon the Cross. Believing that Christ died for our sins and that through the celebration of Holy Communion and belief in him we are restored to fellowship with the Father, do you promise to acknowledge and serve him as your Lord and Savior not just in church but in your daily lives?

C: **Yes, and I ask Jesus to help me.**

L: As God supplies seed to the sower and bread for food, so he will bless each of you as you plant the seed of the Word of God in our hearts and share the administration of communion among us. Please kneel and receive God's blessing and anointing for this service.

L: Congregation please stand and let us pray: When Christ ascended on high he gave gifts to his people. We pray now that the Holy Spirit will stir up those spiritual gifts within you and anoint you for the ministry of reading and of assisting with holy communion. Pour out your Spirit, Gracious Lord, on these your faithful servants who now kneel before you. Be with us, as a congregation, in supporting and encouraging their ministry among us. Equip them as saints for the work of ministry, for the building up of the body of Christ until all of us come to the unity of the faith and the knowledge of the Son of God. May the love they have for their Lord and Savior continue to grow as they share with us through service. Be now anointed with the Holy Spirit to minister in our midst as readers and communion assistants in the name of the Father, the Son, and the Holy Spirit.

C: **Amen.**

L: Empowered by the Spirit, go in peace.

Installation Of Council Members

A Service Of Commissioning

L: Today we, as a family in Christ Jesus our Lord, install those whom the Holy Spirit has called to a position of leadership among us. Those who will be serving the Lord as council members, newly elected members and those fulfilling their elected terms, are asked to come forward at this time to be installed for that ministry in our midst.
(Introduction of council members.)

L: Luke tells us in the Book of Acts that, as the number of disciples increased, complaints concerning the care of certain members of the body of believers were being overlooked by the Apostles. Therefore, the Twelve gathered all the disciples together and said, "It would not be right for us to neglect the ministry of the Word of God . . ." In order to respond to the needs of the people, they were asked to choose from among them disciples of Christ who were known to be filled with the Spirit and wisdom. Those chosen were then given certain responsibilities to fulfill in order that the Apostles could carry out their ministry of prayer and the preaching of the Word.

God has called me, as your pastor, to serve in your midst, carrying out the ministry of Word and sacrament. Along with this comes a wide responsibility of other ministries. In order that the ministry at *(name of church)* might be full and a blessing to all, you have been called and set apart to assist in the leadership of the work of Christ in our congregation.

As elected and called council members, do you promise to be faithful in fulfilling your elected term to this position here at *(name of church)*?

49

C: Yes, and I ask God to help me.

L: Faithful attendance in worship and living out your call not only in church but in your daily life witnesses to the commitment you have made as disciples to Jesus Christ as Lord. Do you promise to let your light shine by your example?

C: Yes, and I ask God to help me.

L: In order to be rooted and grounded in faith, the Apostles diligently studied the Word and devoted their time to prayer. Do you promise to undergird our ministry through prayer and the study of the Word?

C: Yes, and I ask God to help me.

L: Congregation, please rise and bless your members along with me as they are installed for service among us.

All: We recognize your ministry as council members in our midst. God has chosen you to serve him and to carry out your duties that his perfect will will be done in the life of this congregation. We rejoice that he will bless you, and we promise to support you in prayer and to asssit you in our actions in ministry. May God bless and anoint you for this service. In the name of the Father, and of the Son, and of the Holy Spirit. Amen.
(Option: Council members kneel and are anointed with oil by the pastor.)

L: Go in peace, knowing God has blessed you and empowered you for service.

All: Amen.

Installation Of Sunday School Teachers

A Service Of Commissioning

L: The Holy Spirit has called everyone in the church to share their gifts in ministry. Paul tells us that the Spirit gifts individuals in many ways manifesting those gifts for the common good (1 Corinthians 12). One of those manifestations is that of teaching. As the Spirit moves in the life of a congregation, the members of that body are endowed with special gifts which enable them to perform a specific service. They then become gifts themselves. It is God who calls and empowers for Christ's service (Ephesians 4). Nothing is left to mere human judgment or self-choosing.

We take this time today to recognize those in our midst who have answered the call to share in this special ministry with our youth through education. I ask those who will be serving the Lord in the ministry of teaching (teachers and substitutes), the administration of education (Sunday school superintendent), and our youth music instructors (cherub and junior choir directors and accompanist) to now come forward to be installed for those services.

L: ''Jesus went through all the towns and villages, teaching in their synagogues, preaching in their synagogues, preaching the good news of the kingdom and healing every disease and sickness. When he saw the crowds, he had compassion on them, because they were harassed and helpless, like sheep without a shepherd. Then he said to his disciples, 'The harvest is plentiful but the workers are few. Ask the Lord of the harvest, therefore, to send out workers into his harvest field (Matthew 9:35-37).' ''

L: Fellow workers, you stand at the beginning of a new year of tilling and planting the Word of God in the hearts of our youth. Do you promise each week to faithfully prepare for your time of sharing God's teaching and instructions with your classes?

C: Yes, and I ask God to help me.

L: The Word tells us that "students are not above their teacher, nor servants above their master. It is enough for students to be like their teacher, and servants like their master (Matthew 10:24-25)." Do you promise to take time as a student yourself to study personally from the Word of God allowing the Holy Spirit to instruct you?

C: Yes, and I ask God to instruct and guide me.

L: Jesus told us that if we loved him we would obey his teachings (John 14:23). Do you promise to love Christ and be obedient to his teachings and his call on your life?

C: Yes, and I ask God to help me.

L: The Counselor, the Holy Spirit, came from the Father in Christ's name to teach us all things and remind us of everything that Christ spoke to his disciples (John 14:26). As a disciple of Christ, do you promise to call upon the Spirit to guide you in your teaching and to reveal more of Christ to you?

C: Yes, and I ask God to anoint me.

L: Paul told us that unless we have love undergirding the gifts God blesses us with, we become resounding gongs or clanging cymbals. Do you promise to love your students and be patient and kind in your instruction?

C: Yes, and I ask God to fill me with his love.

L: Let us pray. Lord Jesus, look with favor upon those who have responded in love for your service. Anoint and bless them as they instruct your children. Stir up the many gifts each has been given by your Spirit that our body may grow in the knowledge of Christ as Lord. Holy Spirit, be their guide and source of power. May their labors, done in your name, bring forth a rich harvest of souls. We pray in Christ's name.

C: Amen.

L: Go in peace and serve the Lord.

C: Thanks be to God!

Bible Sunday

A Service For Bible Presentation

Psalm 119 tells us that God's Word is eternal; it stands firm in the heavens. As we meditate on God's Word, we grow in our insight and understanding. The Word keeps us headed in the right direction becoming a lamp unto our feet and a light for our path. From it we gain understanding about the direction God wants us to go.

Proverbs tells us to bring up our children in the way they should go, and when they are old they will not depart from it (Proverbs 22:6). God chose his children, Israel, to know his Word. They were to fix his words in their hearts and minds taking every opportunity in their daily living to teach and share the Word of God with their children. At night they were to meditate on them. In this way, God's Word would be handed down from generation to generation (Deuteronomy 11:18-21).

God promises us salvation in Christ Jesus our Lord. We share that good news with our children by introducing them to God's Living Word, Jesus, and to God's written word, the Bible.

The Second Epistle to Timothy encourages us to hold fast to the truth we have been taught through the Word. In prison and abandoned by friends, Paul found great comfort in God's Word and reminded Timothy that from infancy his friend had known the Holy Scriptures, which made him wise to salvation through faith in Christ Jesus. "All Scripture," he states, "is inspired by God and is useful for teaching, rebuking, correcting, and training in righteousness, so that the follower of God may be thoroughly equipped for every good work (2 Timothy 3:15-16)."

We are to place into our children's hands the Holy Scriptures so that they will become wise to God's salvation offered to them in Christ Jesus our Lord. As they read and study God's Word, they will become aware of the grace and love of God poured out for them in Jesus the Christ. As a result of the instruction they receive from the Word, they will be equipped to live godly lives.

It is the privilege of this congregation to present to our third graders a Bible of their own that they may use in their studies at Sunday school and in their personal devotional time at home as well as with their families.

As I read the names of those receiving their Bibles today, I ask that they come forward so I may place the Word of God in their hands on behalf of the congregation.

(Children come forward as names are read.)

L: Congregation, as a family in Christ, I encourage you to help our young people through your example and prayer to make the Word of God an integral part of their lives. Witness to them through your use of the Bible, your study, and your life, how sweet God's Word is and how it is the source of our life in Christ.

L: "How sweet are your words to my taste, sweeter than honey to my mouth (Psalm 119:103)!"

C: **"Taste and see that the Lord is good (Psalm 34:8)!"**

L: "Let the Word of God dwell in you richly as you teach and admonish one another with all wisdom, and as you sing psalms, hymns and spiritual songs with gratitude in your hearts to God (Colossians 3:16)."

C: **"I have hidden your word in my heart (Psalm 119:11)."**

56

L: "Finally, whatever you have learned or received from me, or seen in me, put it into practice (Philippians 4:9)."

C: **"Do not merely listen to the Word. Do what it says (James 1:22)."**

L: And all God's people say,

All: Amen and amen!

Honoring The Heart Of Peace

A Service In Remembrance Of Martin Luther King, Jr.

Today we recognize the Reverend Martin Luther King, Jr., a fighter for freedom. As a minister of God and a Nobel Peace Prize winner for non-violent leadership of the American movement for civil rights, Dr. King worked toward fulfilling the mission to which God had called him: a peacemaker. He believed that in the end peace will come from unarmed truth and unconditional love. Looking at the violence and injustice of his day, he put his hope in God for a brighter tomorrow. He dared to dream of a time when society would be at peace with itself. The words of Isaiah the prophet became engraved on his heart: "The wolf will live with the lamb, the leopard will lie down with the goat, the calf and the lion and the yearling together; and a little child will lead them . . . for the earth will be full of the knowledge of the Lord (Isaiah 11:6, 9b)."

HEARTS WOVEN IN PEACE AND HOPE

L: Prince of Peace, we look forward to the day when wounded justice will be lifted up from the dust of shame and reign supreme,

C: **Christ shall overcome.**

L: We remember today a man who dreamed a dream,

C: **Dream your dreams in our hearts, O Lord.**

L: We ask your healing upon the hurts of the past,

C: **Build friendship and understanding.**

L: We grieve over the spilled blood of the innocent who died as victims of racial violence,

C: **Forgive our intolerance toward others.**

L: We take for granted our right to vote, forgetting that others have been robbed of their civil liberties,

C: **Help us to exercise that gift of choice.**

L: We enter restaurants and ride on buses not realizing that others were once denied entry or made to take a seat apart from their brothers and sisters,

C: **Seat us with you in equality, O Lord.**

L: Provide all your children with three meals each day to nourish their bodies,

C: **Feed the hungry, O Lord.**

L: Grant equal opportunity for all people through education and culture to nurture their minds,

C: **Open our minds to your wisdom, O Lord.**

L: Help us to treat each other with dignity and equality, freeing the spirit,

C: **True freedom comes from union with you.**

L: As Dr. King and others marched down the roads of our nation in prayer for justice and in non-violent demonstration,

C: **Keep us on our knees in prayer for peace.**

L: Open new avenues of communication between your people that we may work side by side with others in harmony and love,

C: **May we work at truly being one in spirit as we are one in you, O Lord. Amen.**

L: Let us pray: Almighty God, as Dr. King sought to bring peace to areas where intolerance and injustice reigned, help us to understand your call to peace in our world. Give us acceptance of others so that we might be able to live out our lives in community with those different from us. Enable us to see areas of our lives which have become infected with bigotry and judgment. We shudder in remembrance of that moment in time when all the ugliness of racial prejudice and violence erupted, taking the very lives of those who sought to eliminate hatred and bridge the gap of inequality. Bridge that gap which still exists within our nation and in your people by igniting your love in our hearts. Through your Son, Jesus Christ, we pray.

C: **Amen.**

L: In Christ we all have been freed, freed from sin and freed to see others as created in God's image. Join your heart with mine as we proclaim the words of an old slave song, the words inscriibed on Dr. King's tombstone:

All: Free at last,
   Free at last,
   Thank God Almighty, I'm free at last!

Hearts That Celebrate Freedom

A Service For Independence Day

A CALL TO REMEMBER OUR FREEDOM

L: Gracious God, look upon us now as we celebrate the freedom we have in this nation. History causes us to remember the cost of that freedom. Spirit of Truth, be with us, joining our hearts in thanksgiving as we celebrate our Independence Day.

C: **Come Spirit of Freedom, Amen.**

L: Today we celebrate the freedom secured for us as a nation. The battles waged to win independence and keep freedom cost the lives of many. In that liberty, we now work and worship and live under a government that proclaims "One nation, under God, indivisible, with liberty and justice for all."

We remember that freedom does not come without a cost. In freedom, we proclaim the death of one who died to truly set us free. The battle over sin and death was won at the cost of the life of God's own Son. We were set free at that moment to live under God's kingship, with the government of our lives upon Christ's shoulders. But God does not want us to live out that freedom independent from him. So we pause to celebrate his lordship in our lives and our dependency on his mercy.

TRUE FREEDOM IN CHRIST

L: God established our freedom at creation, giving us a choice to eat of his blessings and be sheltered from the knowledge of evil;

C: **We rejoice and celebrate our freedom to choose.**

63

L: Disobeying God, we came to eat of the forbidden fruit and strife entered our lives;

C: **The battle still rages within us, O God.**

L: God sent Christ, to show us the truth and that truth has set us free;

C: **The strife is o'er, the battle won. Jesus, the Truth, has set us free!**

L: We join those who rejoiced in the Spirit of '76 declaring a free and just nation;

C: **Where the Spirit of the Lord is, there is true freedom.**

L: As citizens of this great nation, we pledge our allegiance to defend and uphold that freedom, a blessing from God;

C: **And as subjects of The Most High God, we owe to God our freedom in Christ.**

IN PRAISE OF FREEDOM

L: Christ has freed us from our sins,

C: **Praise God for our salvation.**

L: He came to set the captives free,

C: **Praise God for our salvation.**

L: We are justified freely by God's grace,

C: **Praise God for our salvation.**

L: For freedom Christ has set us free,

C: **Praise God for our salvation.**

L: If the Son sets you free, you will be free indeed,

C: Praise God for our salvation.

L: Freely, freely you have received,

C: Freely we give God praise for our salvation.

L: Let us pray: Almighty Founder of our Faith, pour out upon our nation and each of us as Americans a true spirit of appreciation for the freedoms we enjoy. We bless you, O God, as we gather in celebration of this Independence Day, and ask your Spirit to move mightily throughout our land. We understand the cost of freedom as we see our freedom purchased in Christ's blood. As the Liberty Bell announced the birth of a nation, so let the angels proclaim our birth as children of God. In Christ who sets us free we pray.

C: Our hearts celebrate that freedom. Amen.

SONG OF LIBERTY

Hearts Yearning To Give

A Service Of Commitment

L: The law of Moses stated that one should not put a muzzle on an ox while it is treading out the grain. Paul questioned, "Is it about oxen that God is concerned in this law?" His answer, no. It is for us and our cooperation in the work of the kingdom of God. As the plowman plows and the thresher threshes, they ought to do so sharing in the vision of reaping together the harvest.

God wants his people to work together to share in the harvest he will provide as they work in cooperation with his plan. As we, as individuals, sow our time, talent, and monies, in the work of Christ in the church, we reap together a bountiful harvest of blessing. We are the hands, the feet, the voice of our Lord in the world around us. The church, this congregation, the pastor, the staff, the programs of outreach in all areas, become reality through your support. We muzzle them when we do not support them with our spiritual and financial response to Christ's call. What we plant in the life of this congregation is important. If we plant sparingly from hearts not totally committed in giving to Christ, we will reap a scant harvest. If we plant bountifully from hearts yearning to praise Jesus by our stewardship, we will reap such a harvest that our coffers and parish will overflow with God's blessings.

And so, today, we call upon the Lord to pour out upon us his spirit of giving so that our hearts will yearn to return unto him that which he has blessed us with in gratitude.

SHARING HEARTS

L: Lord, we are reminded that our hearts at times are centered on ourselves. Fill us with your Holy Spirit that our stewardship of our time, talents and monies may be a response centered in you.

C: **We ask your empowering and guidance for the use of your blessing, Holy Spirit.**

L: Help us to be obedient in our giving so that all people will praise you as we share generously with others in our service and commitment to your work in the church.

C: **We long to serve you as you first served us, Lord Jesus.**

L: Enable us to share our faith in you as Lord and help us to witness to our faith by our financial commitment.

C: **We return unto you for all you have given us, Gracious God.**

L: Receive what we offer now, Almighty God, as we make commitment to you.

C: **We offer up to you, O Lord, our commitment of love. Amen.**

(Opportunity to present commitment cards before the Lord. Plates may be passed/congregation may come forward as individuals/families and place cards on altar or into a large basket.)

STEWARDSHIP SONG

L: Paul reminds us that the Lord loves a cheerful giver which is a response of praise and thanksgiving. We continue to pray that God will take our hearts and make them generous so we will be blessed with happiness in the life of this congregation. In love, we have responded to the Spirit's call. In love, we have made our commitment to Christ Jesus our Lord. In love, we go forth to share with the family of God from hearts yearning to bless because we have truly been blessed.

C: **Take our hearts and let them be consecrated unto you, Almighty God. Amen.**

Hearts Celebrate The New Year

A Service For The New Year

L: We enter into another year celebrating the goodness of our God. As we celebrate this new year, we pause to reflect on the blessings and growth of the past year and the hope and vision for the year to come. We stand at a crossroads between past and future. What a wonderful place for us as Christians to be: our focus on God's love and mercy as we look to the Cross of Christ Jesus our Lord. Let us join our hearts now in celebration of this new year that God has prepared for us, his people.

C: Come celebrate the new year!

WE CELEBRATE GOD'S LOVE

(Litany based on Lamentations 3:22-25)

L: The steadfast love of the Lord never ceases;

C: We celebrate your love, O God.

L: God's mercies never come to an end;

C: We celebrate your grace, O God.

L: They are new every morning;

C: We celebrate each day, O God.

L: Great is your faithfulness, O Lord;

C: We celebrate your promises, O God.

L: Our souls rejoice that the Lord is our portion;

C: We celebrate your fullness, O God.

L: Therefore, our hopes rest in God;

C: **We celebrate your goodness, O God.**

L: The Lord is good to those who wait for him;

C: **We celebrate your timing, O God.**

L: God comes to those who seek him;

C: **We celebrate your presence, O God.**

L: Praise the Lord!

C: **Come celebrate the new year!**

WE CELEBRATE THE NEW YEAR IN SONG

(Litany based on Psalm 149)

L: God puts a new song in our mouths as we praise him for this new year,

C: **Sing to the Lord a new song, sing his praise in the assembly of the faithful!**

L: God made a new covenant with his chosen people, writing his love on their hearts,

C: **Let Israel be glad in its Maker; let the children of Zion rejoice in their king!**

L: The world tells us that what has been will be again, and what has been done will be done again for there is nothing new under the sun;

C: **Let the faithful look to the one of hope; let them sing the joy of salvation!**

70

L: Yet God puts a new heart and a new spirit within us;

C: **And we sing to the Lord his new song!**

L: Let us pray: O God, we sing your praises as we enter a New Year in celebration of our faith in you through Christ Jesus our Lord. Forgive us our past: the broken promises, the misguided actions, the deeds not done, the love not shown. In repentance we turn to the Cross of Christ and receive your forgiveness. Grant us hope for the New Year and a clear vision of your perfect will so that we may continue to celebrate our salvation today and every day of our lives. In your blessed name, we pray.

C: **Amen.**

L: Go forth to celebrate the new year!

C: **We praise the Lord, and celebrate Christ's love! Amen.**

SONG OF CELEBRATION FOR THE NEW YEAR

Hearts One In Christ

A Service Celebrating Unity

L: Today we celebrate our oneness with God and each other through hearts that are one in Christ Jesus, our Lord. Jesus tells us that he is the vine and we are the branches. If we remain united with him, we will bear much fruit. But if we do not live in union with him, we can do nothing (John 15:1-5). As we stay connected to Jesus, we will live in harmony with one another. Our Christian unity, our oneness in the body of believers, comes only from our connectedness to Jesus, the True Vine.

So, let us celebrate our Christian unity now by lifting our hearts as one.

THE WORD SPEAKS OF UNITY

L: The Holy Scripture stresses the importance of unity and its call to us as Christians. Paul prayed that God, who is steadfast and encouraging, would grant his people to live in harmony with one another, in accordance with Christ Jesus. Unity in the community of believers produces a people who are able to glorify God with one voice (Romans 15:5-6).

C: May we glorify you with one voice, O Lord!

L: Israel often strayed from the blessing of unity. Renewal came as its leaders turned the people back to celebrate and honor their oneness in being chosen people of God. God's hand comes upon repentant people, giving them one heart to do his will (2 Chronicles 30:12).

C: May we glorify you with one heart, O Lord!

L: God calls the members of the body of Christ to live in unity with one another. As Christians, we witness our union with Jesus as we work and live with one another in unity of spirit through the bond of peace (Ephesians 4:1-3).

C: **May we glorify you with one spirit, O Lord!**

L: God grants gifts to equip the members and build up the body so that all will come to a unity of faith and to a knowledge of the Son of God, mature, attaining the fullness of Christ (Ephesians 4:11-13).

C: **May we glorify you with one faith, O Lord!**

L: Clothing ourselves as one body with the virtues of compassion, kindness, humility, gentleness, patience and forgiveness, we witness to our unity through love which binds everything together in perfect harmony (Colossians 3:12-14).

C: **May we glorify you with one love, O Lord!**

L: Let us pray: Jesus Christ, help us to remain attached to you so we will bear much fruit. Pour out your spirit of unity that we who profess faith in you might witness to that belief by our thoughts, words, deeds and love shown for you and each other. As we are one in the Spirit so shall we be one in the Lord.

C: **With one heart we pray. Amen.**

THE BLESSING OF UNITY

(Litany of Praise based on Psalm 133)

L: How very good and pleasant it is when Christians live together in unity!

C: **We rejoice in our oneness in Christ!**

L: It is like the precious oil on the head, running down upon the beard, on the beard of Aaron, running down over the collar of his robes.

C: Anoint us with the oil of your Spirit and clothe us in unity, O Lord.

L: It is like the dew of Hermon, which falls on the mountains of Zion.

C: Pour out the living water that we may be refreshed as the body of Christ.

L: For there the Lord ordained his blessing, life forevermore.

C: Gathered as your children into one family through Christ, we celebrate the wonderful blessing of everlasting life. Amen.